I Am The Ocean

I Am The Ocean

A Journey from Darkness to Light

MICHAELLE S. SALVADOR

PALMETTO
P U B L I S H I N G
Charleston, SC
www.PalmettoPublishing.com

Copyright © 2024 by Michaelle S. Salvador

All rights reserved

No portion of this book may be reproduced, stored in a retrieval system, or transmitted in any form by any means–electronic, mechanical, photocopy, recording, or other–except for brief quotations in printed reviews, without prior permission of the author.

Paperback ISBN: 979-8-8229-5491-5

Dedicated to my sister Gina;

Just when she thought her world was over she became a butterfly.

Contents

Six days 1	Smile (A)...................... 43
Choices 3	Art and Chaos 45
Loneliness 5	Honey Words 47
Pain........................... 7	My worst enemy 49
Cloak 9	Rejected....................... 51
Trying......................... 11	Un-Broken Heart 53
Some Days 13	Whiskey Eyes 55
Stranger....................... 15	In Another Life 57
Ugly Girl 17	The Sun 59
Keeping it in................... 19	Carry me to Shore - (K & A) 61
Hollow........................ 21	Butterfly Wings (G).............. 63
Insomnia 23	In Retrospect 65
Scars.......................... 25	Brother 67
Suffocating 27	Sunlight (J).................... 69
Womb 29	Marked Hearts (J) 71
Flutters 31	Pendulum 73
Lost 33	Hope.......................... 75
White Shutters................. 35	Ocean......................... 77
Exile 37	My Journey 78
Coming out of the darkness (K).. 39	About the Author 79
Epiphany...................... 41	

Six days

Every day I feel emptier and emptier
Those parts so easily given now cut from me
Will it come back they ask
We hope not they say
Those hushed words
As I lay in bed day after day recovering
My cries come late at night when no one can hear me
Numb
Will I ever feel again

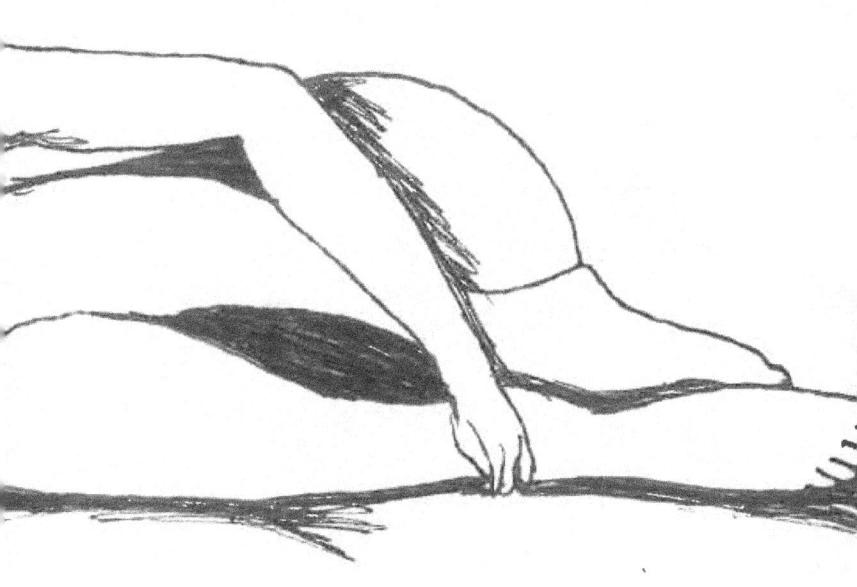

Choices

What choice do I have
Give up, walk away or live
None of the above
It's all a lie
We really have no choice
Facade
Lies
Anger
Yes, those are choices
Another..Trust God

Loneliness

Do I crave the silence
Or have I become indifferent
It's a skill I have mastered to protect myself
Perhaps I have built the walls to my kingdom too high
Is there a way out before the walls begin to crumble into oblivion

Pain

You batter my body daily
Your grip on me stronger than any drug
I take so many pills to keep you at bay
I often lose count
Why do we battle, you and I
A silent understanding
You've brought me this far
I often wonder will you take me to the end

Cloak

It cloaked me so no-one could see
Like a suction it takes me down
I struggle to come up for air
Drowning in the trenches of this invisible ocean
I beg to breathe
Begging who, I don't know
Myself or the demons inside my head
How long will this go on
Until the darkness feels like home
And the light no longer warms me

Trying

Today I went out
But I cried
I don't know why
Perhaps because the pain is consuming me from the inside out
Or maybe its's the loneliness
I simply cannot escape this despondence
At least I tried

Some Days

Some days the mountain seems too tall to climb
She wishes the entire bed would devour her whole
But alas she must pull herself towards the sun
Today she faltered a little
Maybe tomorrow won't be as bad and she won't want
disappear into thin air

Stranger

Why do I feel like a stranger to myself
Like we've never met
My mind is grey and cloudy
Trying to recall who I once was
Do I even want to
Or do I remain in this existential existence

Ugly Girl

Why do I avoid mirrors
Telling myself I'm not good enough
Pinching the excess skin wishing it would disappear just like me
I paint the makeup on day after day
A mask to hide the sorrow
When will I feel pretty

Keeping it in

I swallow my words
Just so you won't know
The battles that wage inside of my head
The voices that scream for me to give up
Fine, good, ok
Those words so easily flow from my mouth
Instead I keep all the scary things hidden and locked away
Silently dying

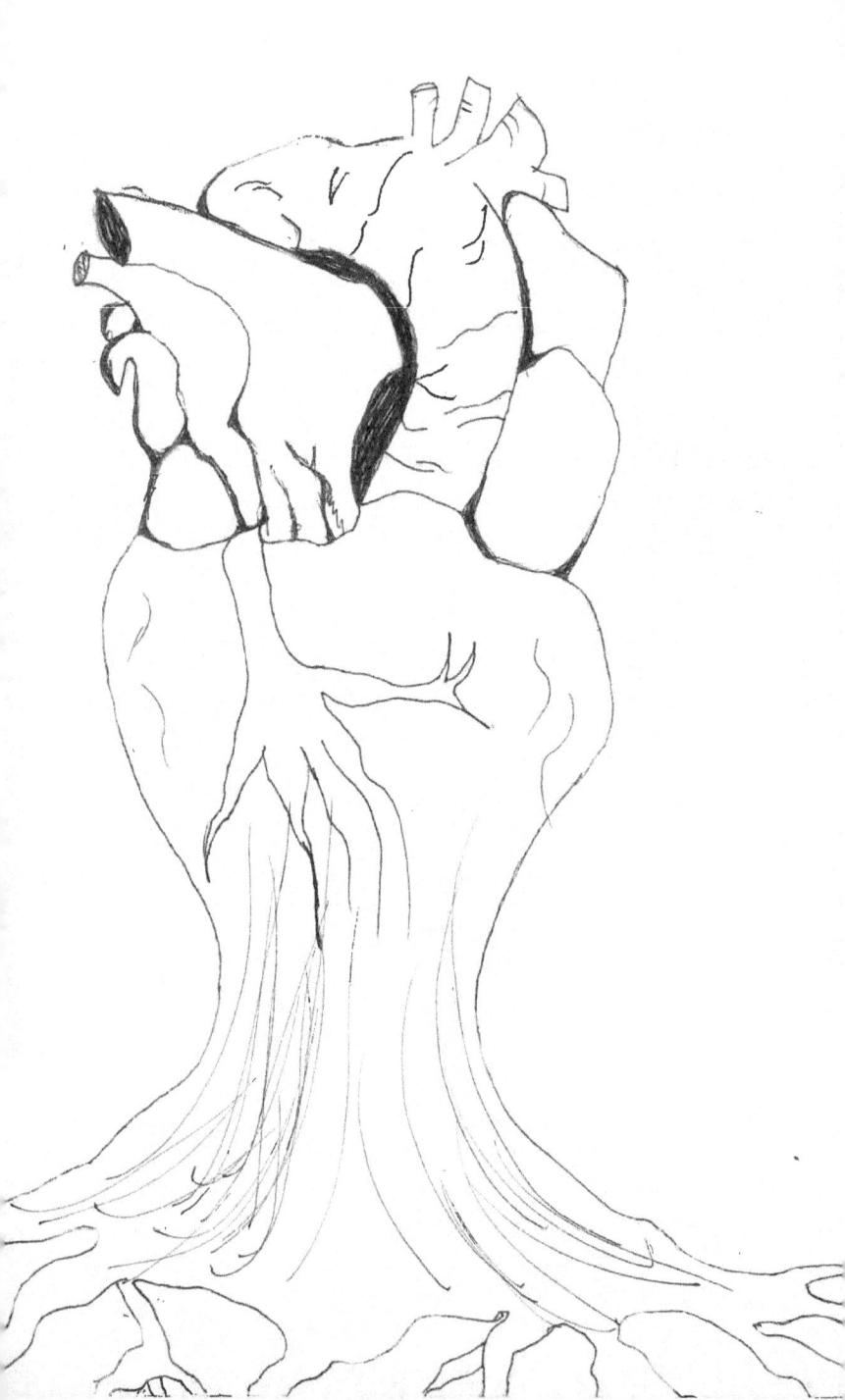

Hollow

I often wonder if my heart will be hollow at the end
When you don't love is it emptied out
I feel it beginning
Maybe it's not so bad
Being apathetic
Like a beautiful carved tree
Hollowness is not emptiness

Insomnia

I lay here night after night begging for the pills to take me
But it never comes
So I write of pain and melancholy
Sleep still alludes me as does love
I wonder what they would both be like
To fall so deeply , I'd dare not wake
But alas I'm here and neither is true

Scars

I look in the mirror
Bruises healing
Soon the incisions will become scars
How close they are to the old ones. Overlapping it seems
My body is a mosaic of wounds that tell a horror story
That may never heal
I wonder will it ever be held in the arms of a lover

Suffocating

The walls are closing in on me
Everyday I stare at the same four walls
Wondering if this is all there is
Am I going to die here
The same walls I built to protect myself
Have become my prison
When will all this end

Womb

My womb has been torn from me
Like the child that never was to be
My loss no one can comprehend
So I hold my agony inside
Uncertain of a future I did not choose

Flutters

Fluttering of wings on parts no longer inside of me
Healing of burned off blackness
The flutters come and go
Feigning womanhood and my fruitful purpose here
on earth

Lost

So much lost to the disease that has ravaged my body
A never ending story
One spent with countless hours in hospital waiting rooms and the acrid smell of death
The utter mastery you have over my life is honestly jaw dropping
Hats off to you

White Shutters

I dreamt of a house with white shutters
With a wrap around porch and kids playing in the yard
Their voices calling my name
Momma, Momma
Laughing they run towards me
I embrace them with all the love I have ever known
I wake up
Remembering ... that life not longer exists for me

Exile

I have exiled myself to this island
Pushing everyone away from me
Desperately hoping one of them will stay
Internally screaming
SEE ME , SEE ME
Yet no one does
Exhausted
I can't do this anymore…

Coming out of the darkness (K)

She is the light I swore to protect
That light now dimming
Its time for reckoning
Her call that saved me
She'll never know
Its time now to come out of the darkness

Epiphany

The waves hit me today
Awoken from the slumber I've been under
They beckoned from the depths towards the shore
Or was it God
Whispering to me
Its time, I've been waiting for you

Smile (A)

Her smile draws me from the edge
Her laugh infectious
My heart is withering but she's keeping it whole
Her beautiful soul does not know how much she heals me
When she says "Auntie I love you"

Art and Chaos

He saw me that way
Between Art and Chaos
They all did, always excited for the chase
A puzzle to solve
Each one of them walked away
Or perhaps it was me who pushed

Honey Words

Tell me how long it took for you to stop loving the version of me you built inside your head
Honey words so easily drip from your mouth
Please tell me the ways you love me
Do you fear me
Or will you leave before you see the real me

My worst enemy

The thoughts I have
They run rampant in my head
Over and over
Sometimes I can't stop them
The mind I use for good turns against me
It has become my own worst enemy
Repeating the cycle I'm trying to break
Creating havoc in my life
When will it cease to exist

Rejected

A verb; to fail to show affection or
concern for someone; rebuff
That verb has en prisononed me for my entire life
It seems I continue to inflict this agony by choosing
those who continue to harm me
Why do I like the pain so much
Am I a Machochist
I'm only aware of how in the aftermath it feels like
a thousand tiny cuts

Un-Broken Heart

The realization my heart is not broken
It's merely been asleep, dormant
Waiting to wake from this slumber
Though its weak
It's healing
The blood still flows
Hope still reigns

Whiskey Eyes

Your eyes deepest amber
Like the whiskey that burns my throat
I think of you that way
A slow burn, that keeps me wanting more
Even when I know its bad for me
Do I walk away or hope for more

In Another Life

When I'm laying awake at night I think of you
Us in another life
We would meet somewhere
Our gazes would connect
You would smile at me
And I would choose you

The Sun

I am reaching towards the sun now
It's beginning to warm my soul once again
Ever so slightly , I'm coming back to life
If I keep my eyes up towards the sky
Maybe I'll be ok

Carry me to Shore – (K & A)

They carry me to shore with their love
Smiles and laughter
Luminescence energy
It shrouds out the darkness
These beautiful souls are vessels of light for the world to see
They scarecly know how they have come to exist as heroes
in mine
Shine bright my sweet girls

Butterfly Wings (G)

You are tattooed on my skin as a reminder
The depth of sadness that weighs on these butterfly wings
is heavy
But as I look into the sky I see you in shades of lavender
You say to me "don't be sad"
For I am free

In Retrospect

I think of how I opened my door and heart to each one of them
Knowing I wasn't the one
Lying there wishing for more
Than a few embraces and kind words
If just to feel something for just a moment
Oh the fairytales we tell ourselves
When we ache for something we cannot describe

Brother

Tied together by blood
But most of all by love
Do you even see what kindness you have
You hold place in my broken heart few ever will
When I look at you I see the little boy running in fields of gold with our sister
Laughing freely
Bub don't lose hope
For you are loved more than you will ever know

Sunlight (J)

The moment I saw you and your eyes met mine
It felt like Sunlight surrounded me
Little did I know this entire time
I have been waiting for you
My breaths are slower now and my heart beats faster
You feel like home
I'm finally at peace

Marked Hearts (J)

Marked Hearts
With fingerprints of many
That's how we are connected
Marked and scarred by others
Those that made us bleed
So deep we didn't know if we would ever recover
Yet, here we are tangled together in his web
Attempting to cleanse ourselves of the past
Praying to know love in its entirety

Pendulum

If I swing a little bit to the other side of the pendulum
Will I fall
The feelings of fear and happiness balanced
They are one and the same
I dare not slip up
I may end up back where I was
So I hold onto this moment like there is no tomorrow

Hope

I cling fast to you
You are my refuge from the storm
Oh how it's almost destroyed me
But I look towards the future, take a breath
Repeat over and over
Faith over Fear
Faith over Fear ...

Ocean

Maybe I'm the ocean in all of this
I've never looked at it that way
This entire journey
Fighting myself
Believing I was being pulled down by an invisible force
When all along it was me
I'm the ocean
I DECIDE my story
I can choose life
But most of all I can learn to love myself

My Journey

I have always dreamt of writing a book, of my travels or perhaps a Vanity Fair version of my life. But as I laid in bed after four surgeries almost back to back due to Endometriosis and side affects from it. I fell into a deep depression and writing became my only solace. At the time I was working through serious mental and physical health issues, slowly cutting myself off from the outside world. My mind overflowed with dark thoughts that when I was able to format them became cathartic. This body of work walks you through the depths of my mind, body and soul. However, not only the poems give insight to when I struggle with self esteem and being alone there are moments of joy. It's a journey from the first poem written to when I began to become healthier. Like many who suffer with illnesses, my hope with sharing my poems is to show people they are not alone. I invite you on this journey with me and my wish is it may serve as an inspiration for anyone who are facing their own struggles. This has transformed my life forever and I will continue to share my experiences with you for as long as possible. I am honored to share my journey and poems with you.

Thank you!

About the Author

Michaelle Salvador, a Colorado native, is a passionate author with degrees in Political and Behavioral Sciences and a certification in Early Childhood Development. Her love for writing, manifested through her first book of poems, *I Am The Ocean*, was born out of a cathartic journey. Beyond writing, she enjoys traveling and cherishing moments with her family and friends. Currently, she is working on her second book, whilst co-hosting a podcast, Transformative *Talk*, with her niece Kailey. Her works resonate deeply with teen girls, women of all ages, and individuals grappling with mental or health issues.

Illustrations by Kailey E. Salvador, a self taught 15 year old artist from Colorado.

www.ingramcontent.com/pod-product-compliance
Lightning Source LLC
LaVergne TN
LVHW051957060526
838201LV00059B/3702